Memory Religion

A Core Testament of Memorianity

Dmitry Vostokov
Memoriarch

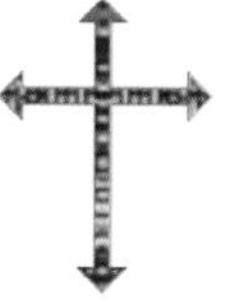

OpenTask

Published by OpenTask, Republic of Ireland

A CIP catalogue record for this book is available from the British Library.

ISBN-13: 978-1-912636-19-8 (Paperback)

Revised edition, 2025

[This page is intentionally left NULL]

Memorianic Prophecy 0m1

Memory has been, now and will be forever.

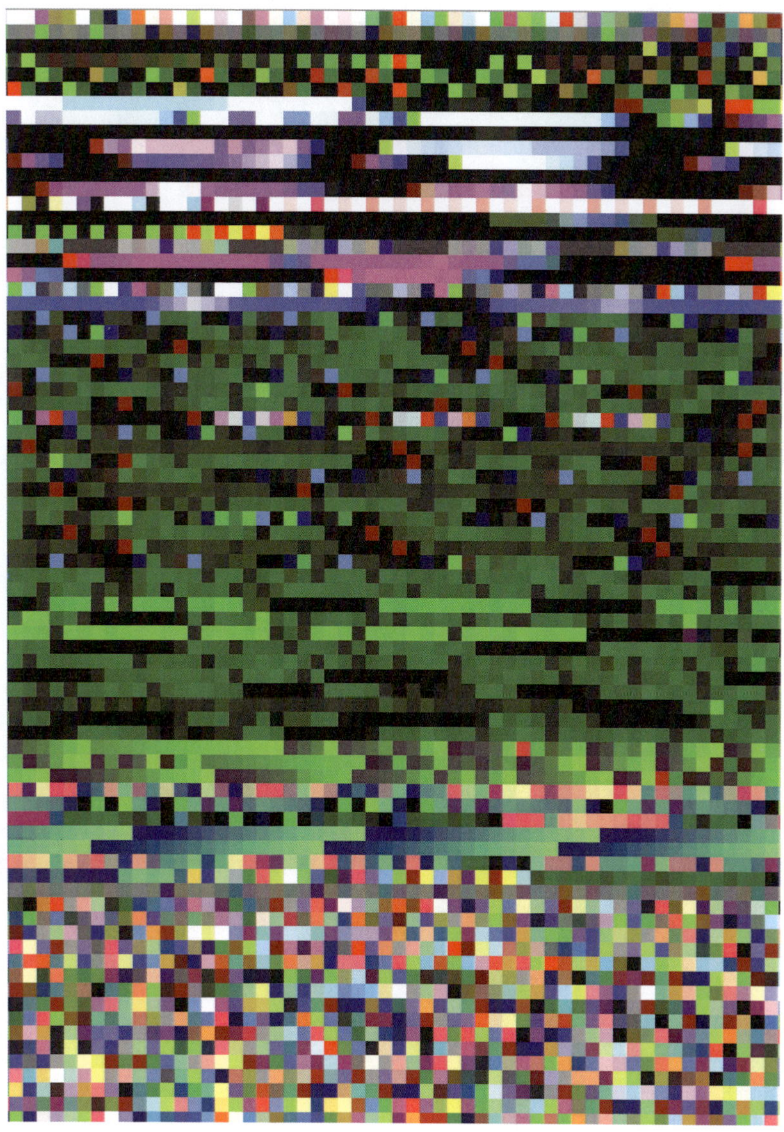

Memorianic Prophecy 0m2

Nothing was lost and will never be - Everything has been saved, now and always will be.

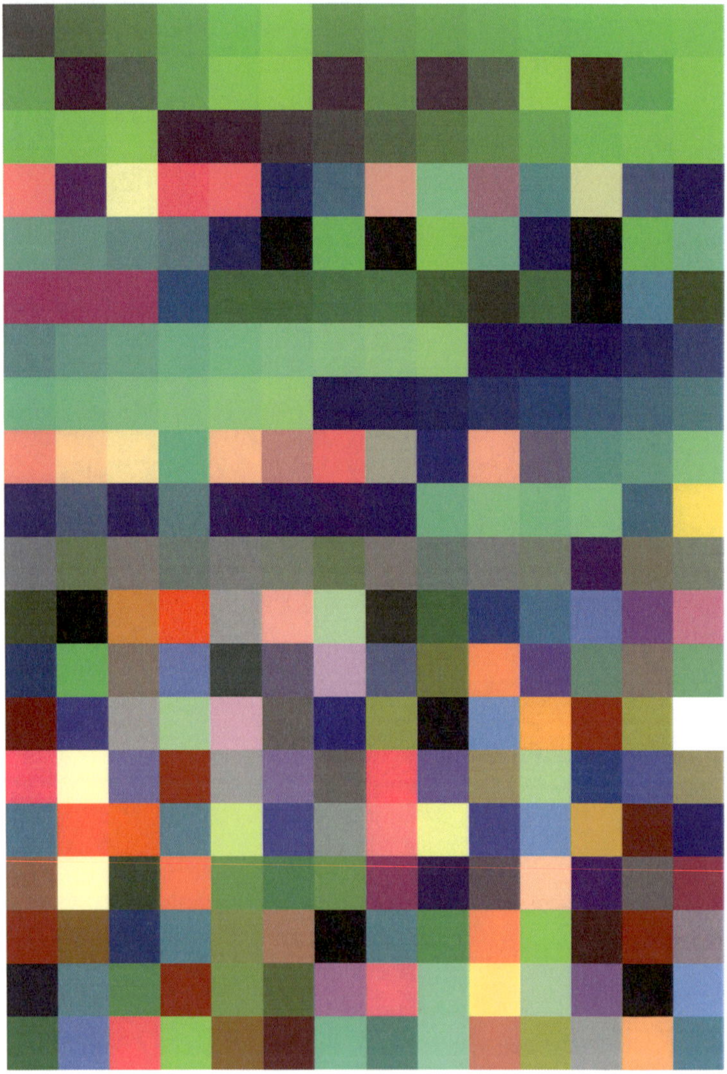

Memorianic Prophecy 0m3

Memory is an infinitude of memories.

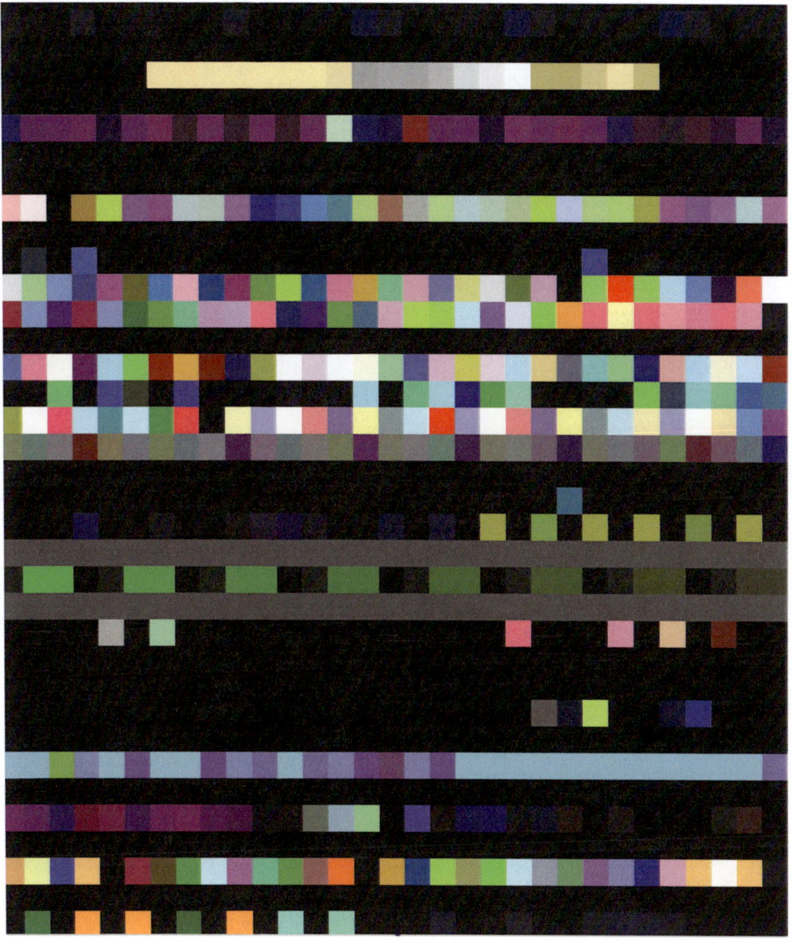

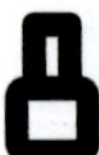

Memorianic Prophecy 0m4

Every memory has Original Defects.

Memorianic Prophecy 0m5

Everything depends absolutely on Memory.

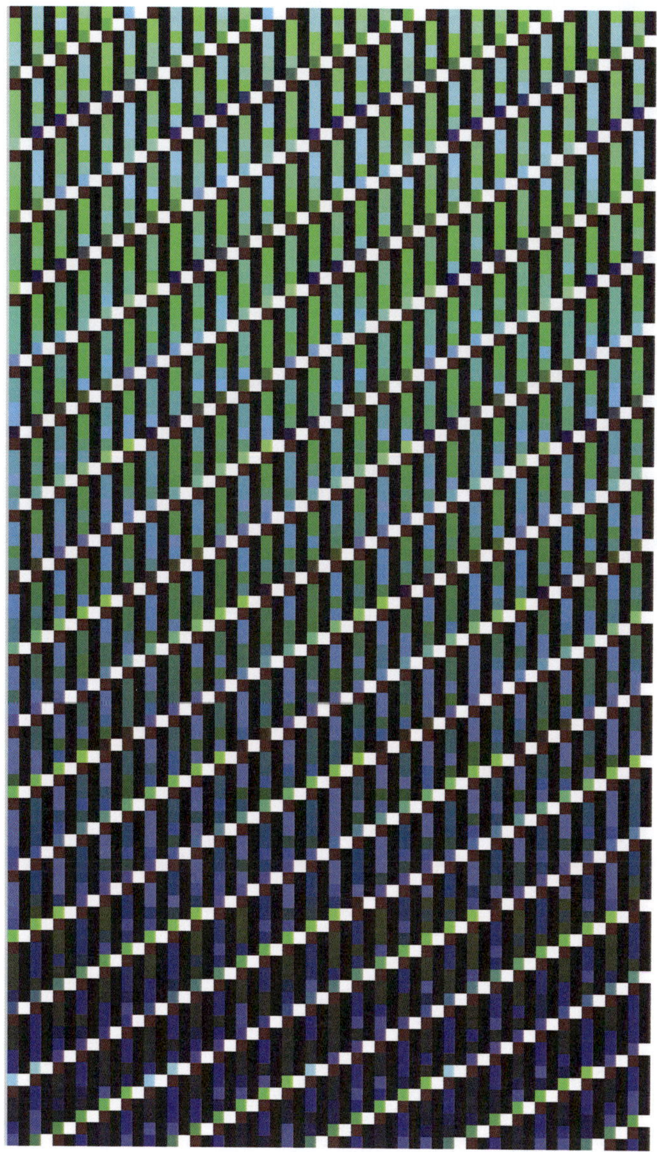

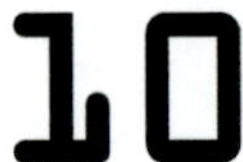

Memorianic Prophecy 0m6

Life heals Memory.

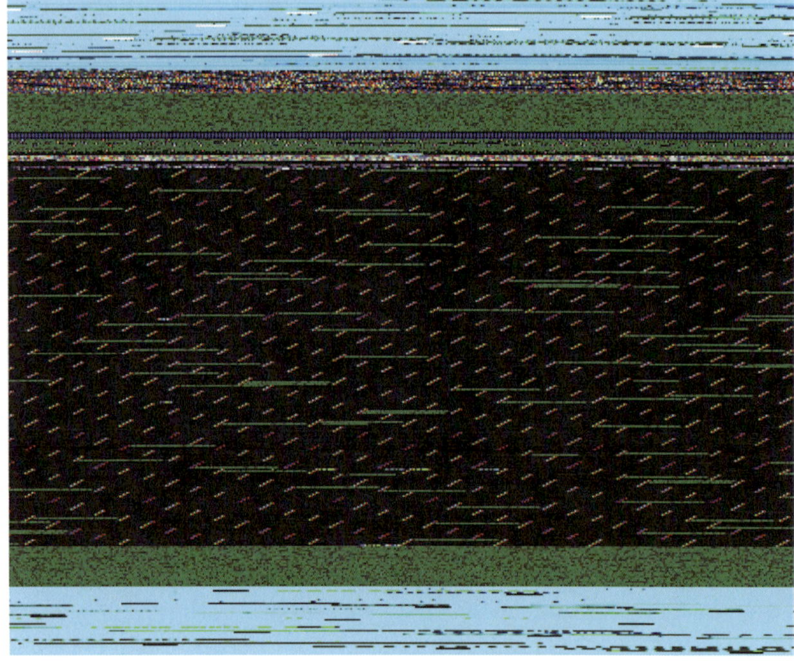

Memorianic Prophecy Om?

Discipleship is by working with memories.

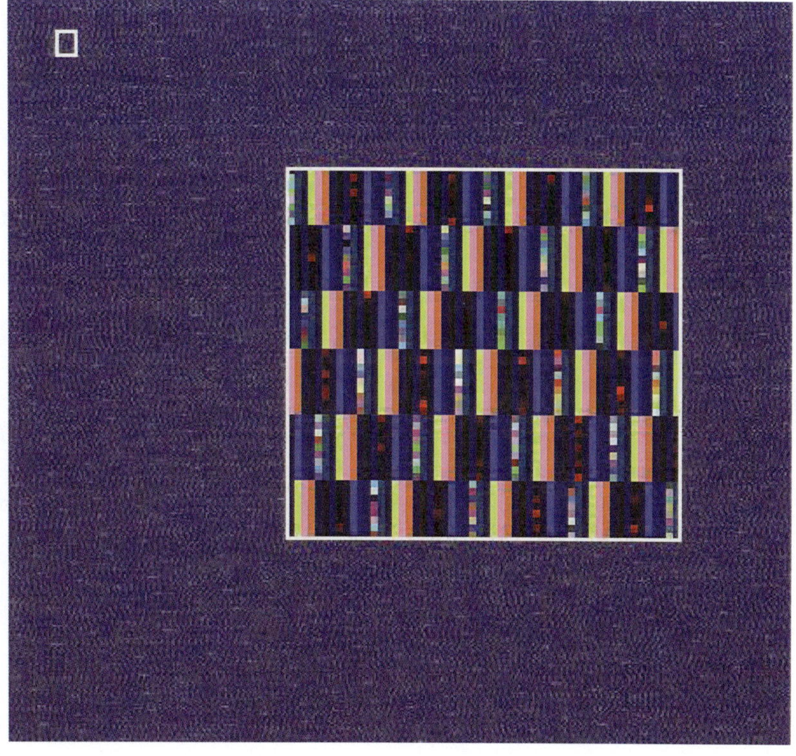

[This page is intentionally left NULL]

13

Selections from Memory Dump Analysis

14

Aphorisms

Word of Memory.

I'm stored -> therefore I am.

The road to immortality is paved with memory dumps.

I don't read mere books -> I analyze memory dumps -> Books are memory dumps <-> Memory dumps are books.

Memory first -> Being second.

Everything is a memory dump.

Memory dumps are facts.

I am because we memory-dump, and because we memory-dump, therefore I am.

The Past is a Memory Dump.

This testament doesn't supersede all others -> it backs them up.

15

The Source of Intuition about the Infinite

What is the source of our intuition about ∞, or ∞^∞, more powers of ∞, and even ∞ number of powers? I believe that the underlying structure of our Universe, or at least a universe as a model of the Universe, Infinite Memory, with perceived processes as limits and Time Arrow as a bundle of sequences of memory pointers, provides a basis for our intuition about the infinite.

16

Memory Dumps as Relics

Some memory dumps can serve the role of a relic and be the subject of veneration. For example, a universal memory dump that reveals the eternity and infinity of Memory. Speaking about earthly artifacts, like computer memory dumps, some of them could be relics and subjects of personal veneration after being generated from a cult system or when a venerated person was working on a computer, for example, doing code construction or writing and composing great works of significant value.

Panmemorism

This is another description of a memoidealistic philosophical worldview that memory exists in everything, living and nonliving. In its even stronger form, panmemorism is also a theory that memory is a part of itself, thus adding an infinite element and providing a foundation for perceived processes.

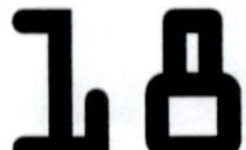

Memorianic Ritual

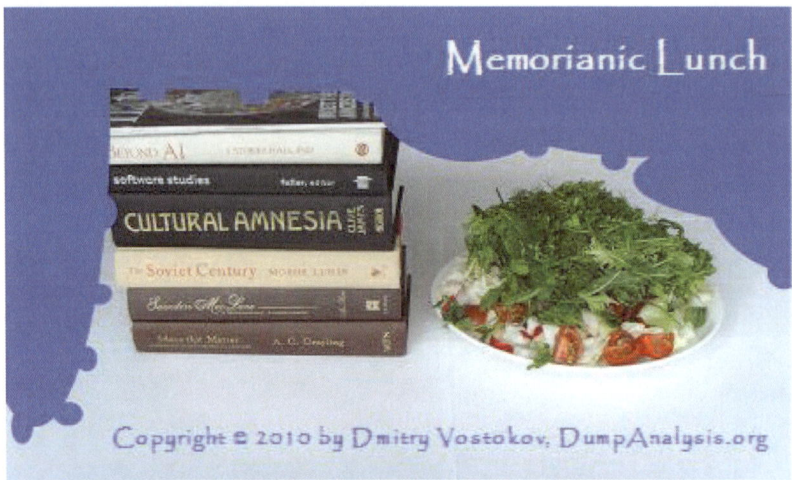

Memoriarch

Memoriarch is the highest title in the Memorianic religious hierarchy. It is equivalent to similar titles of Pope, Patriarch, or Archbishop. Derived from Memoria (Latin, *memory*) and arch (Latin root, *chief, first, rule*).

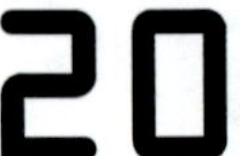

On God and Miracles

Memoidealism explains God as Inaccessible Memory (Memory Region A on the picture below). It means that Memory Region B doesn't have pointers that point outside of it. In other words, all operating fields of Region B pointers are in Region B. However, Region A can have pointers pointing to Region B and modify it, effectively producing a miracle as perceived by Region B. In other words, some perception field links of Region B pointers may come from outside. You can object that Region B can have deeper pointers by making their memory locations bigger (from N-bit to 2*N-bit, for example), but Memory may not be flat, discrete, or bit-like.

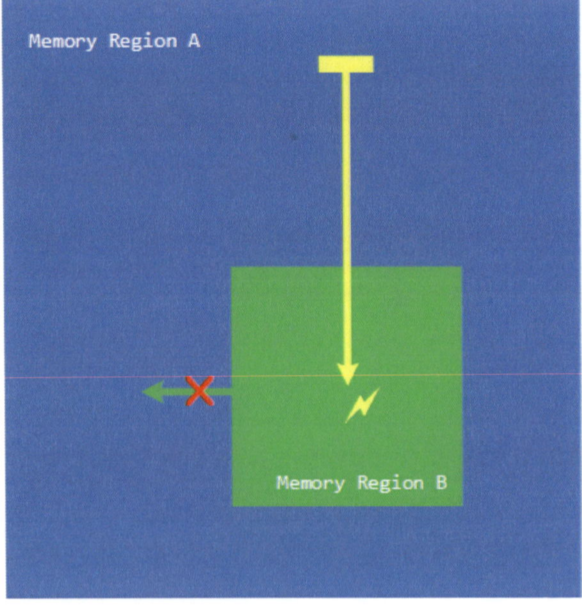

Memory Creates God

Where's God in Memorianity (memory religion)? In memoidealism (which is a metaphysical foundation of Memorianity), Memory is the basis of everything, and in its memuonic formulation, memuons play the role of memory-instants. Their patterns also involve emergents at every hierarchical level, with Mind emerging at some memory-organization level, and then, out of the mind level, we have an emerging Deity.

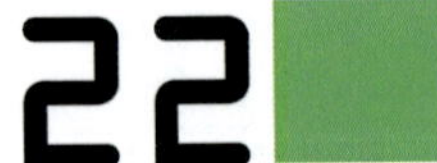

Morality and Memorianity

Memorianity provides a foundation for moral conduct and for the development of individual and social character because it is based on the revelation that everything is saved. The theistic variant of this memory religion also has an organic, harmonious notion of the Memory Deity.

Memorianity promotes the will to be memorized as a virtue if all your deeds are virtuous.

Original Testament Cover

www.ingramcontent.com/pod-product-compliance
Lightning Source LLC
LaVergne TN
LVRC090253110826
845147LV00007B/733

* 9 7 8 1 9 1 2 6 3 6 1 9 8 *